IT'S TIME TO LEARN ABOUT SONGBIRDS

It's Time to Learn about Songbirds

Walter the Educator

Silent King Books
A WhichHead Entertainment Imprint

Copyright © 2025 by Walter the Educator

All rights reserved. No part of this book may be reproduced in any manner whatsoever without written per- mission except in the case of brief quotations embodied in critical articles and reviews.

First Printing, 2024

Disclaimer

This book is a literary work; the story is not about specific persons, locations, situations, and/or circumstances unless mentioned in a historical context. Any resemblance to real persons, locations, situations, and/or circumstances is coincidental. This book is for entertainment and informational purposes only. The author and publisher offer this information without warranties expressed or implied. No matter the grounds, neither the author nor the publisher will be accountable for any losses, injuries, or other damages caused by the reader's use of this book. The use of this book acknowledges an understanding and acceptance of this disclaimer.

It's Time to Learn about Songbirds is a collectible early learning book by Walter the Educator suitable for all ages belonging to Walter the Educator's Time to Eat Book Series. Collect more books at WaltertheEducator.com

USE THE EXTRA SPACE TO TAKE NOTES AND DOCUMENT YOUR MEMORIES

SONGBIRDS

High in the trees or on a wire,

It's Time to Learn about
Songbirds

A songbird sings like a tiny choir.

With chirps and whistles, trills so bright,

They greet the world at morning light.

Robins, sparrows, cardinals too,

Come in colors, red and blue!

Some are yellow, some are brown,

Some wear feathers like a crown!

Their songs can help them find a mate,

Or warn their friends, "Fly! Don't wait!"

Each bird has a tune, its own sweet call,

To chat and chirp, both big and small.

With tiny beaks, they peck and pick,

Eating bugs and seeds real quick.

Some love berries, some like grain,

Some sip nectar when it rains.

It's Time to Learn about
Songbirds

A nest they build, so soft and round,

In trees, in shrubs, or on the ground.

They use some grass, some twigs, some string,

A cozy spot for eggs in spring!

Out pops a chick so small and new,

With fluffy feathers, gray or blue.

Its beak stays wide to get a treat,

As parents bring it bugs to eat.

Some songbirds fly both near and far,

Traveling south past trees and cars.

When winter comes, they go away,

Then find their homes on warmer days.

Their wings are quick, their tails so neat,

They flit and flutter on tiny feet.

Some fly high, some stay low,

It's Time to Learn about
Songbirds

Some hop fast and to and fro!

Listen closely, you will hear,

A songbird's tune so bright and clear.

Morning, evening, all day long,

The world is filled with nature's song!

So when you see one in a tree,

Stop and listen, let them be!

For songbirds bring a cheerful sound,

It's Time to Learn about
Songbirds

That spreads their joy the whole year round!

ABOUT THE CREATOR

Walter the Educator is one of the pseudonyms for Walter Anderson. Formally educated in Chemistry, Business, and Education, he is an educator, an author, a diverse entrepreneur, and he is the son of a disabled war veteran. "Walter the Educator" shares his time between educating and creating. He holds interests and owns several creative projects that entertain, enlighten, enhance, and educate, hoping to inspire and motivate you. Follow, find new works, and stay up to date with Walter the Educator™

at WaltertheEducator.com

www.ingramcontent.com/pod-product-compliance
Lightning Source LLC
LaVergne TN
LVHW051921060526
838201LV00060B/4105